Everything I Couldn't Tell You

Everything I Couldn't Tell You

Jeff D'Hondt

Playwrights Canada Press
Toronto

First edition: February 2024
Printed and bound in Canada by Imprimerie Gauvin, Gatineau

Jacket art and design by Star Daughter Woman

Playwrights Canada Press
202-269 Richmond St. W., Toronto, ON M5V 1X1
416.703.0013 | info@playwrightscanada.com | www.playwrightscanada.com

LIBRARY AND ARCHIVES CANADA CATALOGUING IN PUBLICATION
Title: Everything I couldn't tell you / Jeff D'Hondt.
Other titles: Everything I could not tell you
Names: D'Hondt, Jeff, author.
Description: First edition. | In English, with some text in Lenape.
Identifiers: Canadiana (print) 20230592341 | Canadiana (ebook) 2023059235X | ISBN 9780369104830 (softcover) | ISBN 9780369104847 (PDF) | ISBN 9780369104854 (EPUB)
Subjects: LCGFT: Drama.
Classification: LCC PS8607.H66 E94 2024 | DDC C812/.6—dc23

Playwrights Canada Press staff work across Turtle Island, on Treaty 7, Treaty 13, and Treaty 20 territories, which are the current and ancestral homes of the Anishinaabe Nations (Ojibwe / Chippewa, Odawa, Potawatomi, Algonquin, Saulteaux, Nipissing, and Mississauga / Michi Saagiig), the Blackfoot Confederacy (Kainai, Piikani, and Siksika), néhiyaw, Sioux, Stoney Nakoda, Tsuut'ina, Wendat, and members of the Haudenosaunee Confederacy (Mohawk, Oneida, Onondaga, Cayuga, Seneca, and Tuscarora), as well as Metis and Inuit peoples. It always was and always will be Indigenous land.

We acknowledge the financial support of the Canada Council for the Arts, the Ontario Arts Council (OAC), Ontario Creates, the Government of Ontario, and the Government of Canada for our publishing activities.

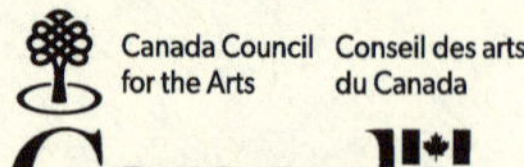

Canada

Ontario

This work is dedicated to the memory of my aunt and uncle, Margaret Lois Webster and Daniel Adaire Webster, whose lifelong passion for theatre became my own. Nàhwàaleew (I love you).

Author's Preface

Everything I Couldn't Tell You was born because I felt dead. To many I seemed alive. Many tumultuous familial relationships had settled into peaceful, loving connections. Thank goodness for everyone I care about. I was a social worker with a leadership role at a prominent Indigenous organization. I'd found a series of cassette tapes containing Lenape lessons I could digitize. I could hear my original language, whenever I wanted to, for the first time in my life. Buoyed by the discovery, I wrote draft after draft of the script. It was my second stage play, ever, and I wanted to blow minds with the text. That opportunity came about fifty drafts into the development process. Why Not Theatre accepted my application to their RISER Festival in Toronto.

These apparent successes hid the underbelly to my life. Anguish co-occurred with success, daily. My pain emerged in the text rather than in my conversations with loved ones. My marriage was crumbling, whatever my partner and I did to repair it. I couldn't tell her what she needed to hear. An anxiety disorder took its toll on my physical and mental health. I couldn't discuss the full extent of what I was enduring, as it involved a harrowing trauma I've only shared with a friend, my ex, a therapist I no longer see, a now deceased Elder, and my mother. I went to ceremonies and therapy for all those years, usually unable to speak plainly to anyone else. And as I did that healing work, grief emerged. Prior to writing this script, I'd experienced loss after loss in the span of only a few years, grief that stuck with me throughout the entire creative process. My dad had died, a Jack Nicholson-like character, gone before we fully made peace. My grandma had also passed, her kindness lost forever. And ill health had claimed my aunt and uncle, to whom this play is dedicated, because they inspired my love of theatre. Each loss birthed agony and intensified my anxiety. My social work career fell apart as my mental and physical health declined. I barely cared. The rest of my life had already crumbled.

Amidst the pain, during a visit with a friend in Vancouver, the final scene of this play came to my mind. A whisper told me to finish the rest of the script, whatever happened with my mental health. I couldn't talk about grief. But I could write about loss. I couldn't talk about my failed marriage. That breakdown became two doctors struggling to help someone who desperately wanted their aid and clearly wasn't getting it. By no coincidence, those doctors are also facing significant career failure. Therapy and ceremony helped me face pain head on; writing supported me in the abstract. And write I did, for five years as I continued to heal. When Alison screams, "Everything doesn't end in pain!" I screamed the same. When Alison and Megan try to heal with language and art, that was me. And I mean *try*. Learning Lenape, my original language, seemed an exciting prospect. At the time of writing there were thirteen fluent speakers. If I could pull off learning a language that rare, what better way to prove I should live?

I failed.

With no easy access to fluent speakers and my life in disarray, the odds against me were too great. I also discovered the lessons were from a dialect not spoken in Canada, so whatever work I'd done that far was for naught. Instead, I found joy hearing the correct dialect through online recordings of stories and reading it in dictionaries. They weren't lessons, yet they moved me nevertheless. Someone, somewhere, knew a language that helped me articulate thoughts once too muddled to touch my heart. The first time I opened an audio file and heard the proper dialect, I was shaken. Imagine falling into the Niagara River, frantic that you won't reach the shore before you go over the falls. For a second, such chaos filled my head. But then I knew what was happening. Everything I'd wanted to say but couldn't was coming up at once. It was terrifying only for a few seconds. Somehow a voice reached me. It told me that part of my silence was the result of only having English to speak. I needed a language that didn't exist to tell me I was crazy, an Indigenous wreck ready to ruin his life. Lenape existed to teach me to heal, whatever my knowledge of it.

I had to stop the recording to go upstairs, tears of relief on my cheek as I collapsed in bed. I remained there for three hours, bawling. While my brain couldn't process the language, my spirit could. Those tears were incredible medicine. Everything I couldn't say was released, without a word. If I couldn't learn the language, my work could still reach the stage, to show others what Lenape can do. It's a river that can carry those in pain to shore, when the strength to swim eludes us. Hence the river Megan and Alison see in the script.

This play exists not to bring the impossible to life. But to acknowledge the pain of getting knocked out. Not down—out. I failed as a husband. As a social worker. And I'd made mistakes as a son, nephew, and grandson that could no longer be atoned for. The people I loved were gone. Some odds can't be beaten. And some of us live on anyway. Some of us. Alison, Cassandra, and Megan lost a sister, a partner, and a grandmother, respectively. They may survive their grief. They may not. What matters is that they lost love they may never replace. Too often we're fed stories about underdogs beating the odds, about hope that might not exist outside a theatre. I've zero patience for platitudes. I want us to witness pain. And to stand by those hurting, even if success is impossible. Because loss and failure are inevitable. Love can be just as inevitable as if we put aside false narratives of hope and stand by each other, outside feel-good stories of inspiration.

In real life oppression and cruelty rob many I love of their healing. Should they beat tough odds, the hateful change the game. There are no words to describe that suffering. And a single question drove me as I wrote: "What lessons can be learned from pain so profound it defies language?" Neither Lenape or English can replace justice and healing. But love might carry a spirit, not to victory or newfound wisdom, but through whatever life we must live.

This is a story for those who keep fighting, even if healing seems out of reach.

Everything I Couldn't Tell You was produced as part of Why Not Theatre's RISER PROJECT from May 4–12, 2018 at the Theatre Centre, Toronto, Ontario, with the following cast and crew:

Cheri Maracle as Dr. Alison Brant/Melanie
Jenny Young as Dr. Cassandra Barry
PJ Prudat as Megan Cornelius

Director: Erin Brandenburg
Dramaturg: Emma Mackenzie Hillier
Stage Manager: Jordana Weiss
Set Design: Michel Charbonneau
Lighting Design: Andre du Toit
Costume Design: Isidra Cruz
Sound Design/Composition: Andrew Penner
Assistant Sound Design: Deanna H. Choi
Videographer: Tess Girard
Fight Director: Simon Fon
Production Manager: Pip Bradford
Technical Director: Steph Raposo
Producer: Jeff D'Hondt
Assistant Producer: Michelle Langille

Playwright's Notes

Language: The Lenape used herein is not the true language. Grammatical errors, incorrectly mixed dialects, misspellings, and poorly chosen vocabulary abound to the point the language is gibberish. The language has been harmed by colonization; the incorrect Lenape reflects this harm.

Set: Those in Megan's pain cannot focus on details. Thus sets, unless otherwise noted, should be abstractions, highlighted only by a few key elements. Lights, sound, video, text, and mimed environments will build a scene.

Props: Distress makes senses cheat. The real might seem imaginary; the fanciful gains a tactile presence. Thus, some props will be mimed, others will not. The creative team can determine which props have physical presence.

Projections: The wall, the floor, the performers, Lucite screens, or other surfaces may be used for projections. Images are punctures into the spirit world. They amplify thoughts in ways words cannot.

Cast Of Characters

DR. ALISON MONTOUR: Indigenous physician/art therapist, forties.
DR. CASSANDRA BARRY: Settler physician/neuroscientist, forties.
MEGAN CORNELIUS: Indigenous patient, thirties.
MELANIE: Deceased neuropsychologist, thirties, played by Alison.
BERNARD: Chief of Medicine, fifties.

Setting

Various locations in Castle Dawn, Ontario, present day.

At rise:

The struggle to turn damage into salvation commences as the audience enters a Lenape Big House (an exact replica must not be used to respect the sacredness of the space). The building resembles a massive log cabin crossed with a longhouse. It feels like a place of ritual, until they enter it.

Inside, they gather in a mock Victorian medical theatre. They observe the performance from the risers, forcing them to use a colonial gaze. The entrance to the risers is located on the west. A wall frames the north, with a section of scrim. East and south are filled by the risers. All structures frame an operating theatre on the floor. The space might help someone heal, if unease doesn't compel them to flee.

Prologue

Lights up on a tacky convention centre: if you speak here, your career will die.

DR. ALISON MONTOUR, Indigenous, forties, begins her presentation. She wears an EEG headset. Her smile, faint as it is, hints she'll be an instant friend. Her threadbare vintage clothing suggests she'll need a loan. No one would guess she's a physician and scientist.

PROJECTION (FredSpeaks logo): A spinning globe flips, revealing a slogan: "Small world, big ideas." Blink. It's gone, like her pride. Her brain scan appears. It glows green, red, and yellow.

ALISON: I'm Dr. Alison Montour. I normally use Lenape to say my nation, my clan, and my name. But you can see my brain scan. I don't want to speak my language. Until you understand how it changes me.

Thirteen fluent speakers of Lenape remain. They speak our original words; they also think with them. An additional one hundred of us, myself included, are near fluent. We speak Lenape but we think in English. Words like drunk and whore. Words beaten into us by colonizers.

Lenape is medicine. It calms us. It tells us how to love, how to think kindly of ourselves. I scanned my brain, to see our language soothe my cells.

When I spoke Lenape, I used neural pathways unattached to trauma. Our language freed me; the images proved it. That peace was always undone. My thoughts returned to English. And the agony it's conditioned me to feel.

Dr. Cassandra Barry revolutionized the treatment of brain injuries. I adapted her work with music and electrical stimulation to break traumatic cycles.

She points at her brain scan. It turns pure red.

Green demonstrates peace. Other colours indicate distress.

PROJECTION (hallucination, river): The current rips across the stage. It slams into her. The sound of rapids blends with the choking breath of a panic attack.

The projection of the river ends.

But her panic continues.

Excuse me.

She flees.

1. Puh-maa-soo-hay-loo-wah [A Reason to Live]

ALISON's cheap, tiny loft proves even doctors can go broke. Half-assembled EEG technology ready for a dumpster covers her second-hand furniture. The refuse tumbles as she rushes to a digital piano connected to a laptop.

She gasps, still seized by panic.

She somehow connects her EEG headset to the piano with trembling hands.

She pounds the laptop.

SOUND: The computer squawks.

A light illuminates the scrim from behind, revealing the balcony scene from Romeo and Juliet. *A silhouette climbs on the balcony's edge, rather than calling out to her lover.*

ALISON batters the computer. Squawk, squawk, squawk.

ALISON: Calibrate, damn it.

The silhouette leaps to her death.

Stephanie.

Wham! ALISON punches the computer.

PROJECTION (brain scan): It lights up, awash in red. Click.

Agony.

PROJECTION (brain scan): A brief flash of yellow pulsates through the otherwise ceaseless red.

Click.

Agitation.

She fights for her breath.

Calm.

PROJECTION (brain scan): The waves of red continue, with another brief pulse of yellow.

Calm, please.

Deep. Breath.

PROJECTION (brain scan): A flash of green. Click.

SOUND: A soothing electronic ping.

(to computer) Calibration successful, jackass.

Click.

SPLIT-SCREEN PROJECTION (brain scan/video): A recorded ALISON smiles like a comforting therapist, side by side with her brain scan.

(in video) Every time you do the procedure, the river feels more like medicine.

On stage, ALISON *plays Rachmaninoff's Piano Concerto No. 2 in* C *Minor, 2nd Movement on the digital keyboard.*

(in video) Steph stood on the edge of her balcony. I couldn't scream. I just watched her jump. She was alive when I reached her. I hugged her, bawling. I couldn't find the words to help her, all those years she was depressed. I couldn't find the words to keep her from jumping. And there was nothing I could tell her now. It was February. Our breath turned to steam. It mixed together. And disappeared. She was gone. She was my sister. I should've known what to say.

On stage, ALISON *plays on.*

(in video) Ke-teh-la-meh mi-pi-sun. [Everything has a balance.]

SPLIT-SCREEN PROJECTION *(scan/video):* ALISON *turns into a cartoon. She kneels in the snow, holding her sister's hand. Her breath turns to steam. Words form inside it: "Nàhwàaleew: I love you."*

(voice-over, in video) Neh-nu-su-mell. A-luh-shi wi-cheh-muck-ween. [I held her hand. That's the only medicine she had left.]

SPLIT-SCREEN PROJECTION *(brain scan/video): Streaks of green and yellow pierce the red.*

On stage, ALISON *sobs with relief.*

2. Twinkle, Twinkle Little—

A fancy doctor's office in a shiny hospital.

DR. CASSANDRA BARRY, forties, a physician and scientist with the sneer of someone smarter than most physicians and scientists, braces for the worst of a therapy session turned storm.

MEGAN CORNELIUS, thirties, a brain-injured Indigenous hurricane, makes white knuckle fists in lieu of strangling CASSANDRA. A letter is stuffed in MEGAN's bra, in plain sight.

CASSANDRA: I assume it's some kind of personal correspondence. I thought you might want to discuss it. Given you have it on prominent display.

MEGAN: Doctors shouldn't stare at my tits.

CASSANDRA: You've baited another argument. To prevent us from discussing something upsetting.

MEGAN: We both know it's coming. The punch. The punch. Trauma, trauma, yak, yak. Scars don't mean as much as healing.

CASSANDRA: If you don't face the reason for those scars—

MEGAN: You're like a kid. Playing a song week after week, just to piss up the same note. Twinkle, twinkle, little—damn, they never get it right. You win. From now on, all we talk about is me getting hit. Until practice makes perfect.

CASSANDRA: Yet again, you're distorting my therapeutic intentions.

MEGAN: He was between me and the door. I couldn't get out. Boom.

He was between me and the door. I couldn't get out. Boom. He was between—

CASSANDRA: Megan, please.

MEGAN: When someone says ouch like me, they heal like me. I want a Native doctor. Who doesn't torture me.

CASSANDRA: The hospital's Elder remains available, however reluctant you—

MEGAN: For the tenth frickin' time, Uma told me never to see one. Or God would cry. City girls need fancy city medicine.

CASSANDRA: I hear the hospital's latest Indigenous social worker—

MEGAN: I put the last two on sick leave. I'll crap gold nuggets before another under-trained fool does me any good. Give me a doctor.

CASSANDRA: The more you narrow the field of potential helpers, the more you sabotage your recovery.

MEGAN: Push my button again. Please.

CASSANDRA: Don't make me call security.

MEGAN: Ke-hu-loo-neh-soo-wa?

CASSANDRA: I didn't catch that.

MEGAN: Ke-hu-loo-neh-soo-wa? Find a doctor who can answer. Or I'll sue.

3. Ne-joos [My Friend]

A bright hospital music-therapy room: cheesy art depicts anthropomorphic music notes dancing like drunken idiots.

MEGAN rushes to the art. She checks for witnesses. Whack, she hammers a mimed baseboard. And retrieves a whisky bottle.

She swills with sweet relief.

She nearly chokes. Someone's here.

MEGAN: Here's a thought. Don't tell staff about my booze. That's not a threat, if you do the smart thing.

I didn't mean to sound—intense. I'm not—me. Maybe you get it. You wouldn't be here if you weren't hurt too.

You look lost. Newbies always are. Turn left. Then right. Then left again. Cass-hole's office is six doors down. Her patients are brain injured. So the genius makes us find her in a maze. Fuuuuccckkk. Have a sip. She's easier to take, if the edge is off.

She offers booze.

Damn, newbie, you're missing out.

(swills) You think I'm a boozy idiot. "Wah. I wanna kill myself. Drinking helps me go numb." If that's where my story stopped, call me a boozy idiot. I've found something that keeps me coming. The best whisky ever made. Stashed right here, nowhere else. I can only enjoy it before and after therapy. Strategy, newbie. Trust me, you'll need one.

Wait until you meet Cass-hole. Don't call her Cassandra. That's a pretty name. She doesn't deserve it. "Aw, you got punched. Poor baby. Tell me more. Tell me." She's lucky I fired her ass. Before I bounced her face off the floor.

That was nasty. I really am a sweet girl. I have references.

She pats the letter in her bra.

Trudy thinks I'm gold, woo hoo.

Maybe your brain's too injured to get a joke. Normal people don't stuff references in their bras. It's a letter. I got it last week. It cheers me up when I—and things got intense again. I'm a good one. I promise. Drink.

She offers booze.

To hell with that camera. It doesn't catch this corner. The rent-a-cops patrolling the place won't fix it without a raise. Cheers.

She offers booze again.

4. Ma-ta-huh-pew-wuh [The Prick]

An office befitting an arrogant prick. Everything pretty in CASSANDRA's space is twice as nice here.

PROJECTION (BERNARD's face): He out-sneers CASSANDRA, hovering over her. He's the medical director, in his fifties. He exists only as a projection, a sarcastic, impersonal jackass born to ensure the practice of medicine is painful.

BERNARD: You've ignored my meeting requests. I'm glad my assistant was able to rearrange your schedule. It's important we talk. I've heard the disturbing news about Megan.

CASSANDRA: She's one case. My success rate is otherwise impeccable.

BERNARD: Yet the smallest mistake mid-procedure could wound someone permanently. That slim margin of error guarantees others will suffer too. These are difficult days. Cuts galore. Some leaders wish to invest in safer treatments.

CASSANDRA: Some. Whose research wasn't funded. Though mine was.

BERNARD: That hurt, Cassandra. These concerns aren't my own. They come from the top. The very top.

CASSANDRA: The very top isn't arguing with me, Bernard. You are.

BERNARD: As Megan argued with you. Until she refused your care.

CASSANDRA: I can still help her.

BERNARD: That's right. Our colleagues mentioned you're looking for an Indigenous physician. With advanced knowledge of brain injuries. Including your procedure. And any complications you overlooked in your haste to justify your funding. Silly me, I forgot they must speak Megan's traditional language. And have the clinical skills to deal with her outbursts. I'm sure you'll find someone with such unique qualifications before opportunists strike. Best of luck, old friend.

CASSANDRA grabs her cellphone, stomping to—

5. *Ma-ta, wok ma-ta [No, Just No]*

CASSANDRA's office: She snarls during a call.

CASSANDRA: *(into phone)* No one you've recommended is even close to adequate. My patient needs help. Now.

I'm well aware Dr. Montour remains available. I made a habit of avoiding her. Long before she ruined her career at FredSpeaks.

I need a gifted clinician. Not an obscure researcher hustling ideas between panic attacks.

And yet we continue to discuss her. I don't care if her distress was an aberration. I can't risk failure. My funding's at stake.

It doesn't matter how many physicians I've brushed aside. There must be someone else.

CASSANDRA hangs up. She charges across the stage as the lights shift. She reaches—

6. *Ke-wuh-cheh-la-too-wuh* *[The Test]*

Star Trek *lab: a technologically advanced medical bay filled with an array of computers, a wildly expensive digital piano, and a mannequin connected to an* EEG *headset.*

ALISON admires the lab, grinning like a child in her first toy store.

CASSANDRA: *(to herself)* Unbelievable.

CASSANDRA taps her foot with impatient frustration. ALISON misses the cue.

ALISON: Holy smokes, any idea that helped my patients was born right here.

CASSANDRA: Dr. Montour.

ALISON: *(distracted)* I've memorized every picture of this place. I don't recognize some of your equipment. You've upgraded.

CASSANDRA: Dr. Montour—

Boom. She smacks a control panel with force that demands attention.

PROJECTION (MEGAN's brain scan): It's pure red.

Your opinion matters more than your admiration.

ALISON: My apologies. I don't mean to gush. I can't believe I'm here.

CASSANDRA: The scan. Please.

ALISON: Yes. Of course.

(reviews it) Whoa. I thought we were discussing a case. This must be a simulation.

CASSANDRA: The brain is quite real.

ALISON: Your patient couldn't function. It's medically impossible.

CASSANDRA: Yet you still must help.

ALISON manipulates the image.

PROJECTION (brain scan): It flips upside down, then sideways and sideways again.

ALISON: Your upgrades have a learning curve.

CASSANDRA sighs in frustration. She manipulates the screen.

PROJECTION (brain scan): The image corrects itself.

She's in her mid-thirties.

CASSANDRA: You don't sound certain.

ALISON: Our discussion feels—unpleasant. If I've done something wrong—

CASSANDRA: My manner will soften if I see your value as a physician.

ALISON: If.

CASSANDRA: My patient needs help I couldn't provide. It remains my task to find her the best care possible. Few meet that standard. Wow me. Identify the reason for her coma.

ALISON manipulates the image.

PROJECTION (brain scan): It turns sideways.

CASSANDRA shakes her head in disbelief. She reaches for the PROJECTION (brain scan): ALISON corrects the image without assistance. It zooms out to a view of the full brain.

ALISON: She suffered a contrecoup. A blow drove her parietal lobe into her skull, contusing it. Her brain rebounded, shredding her frontal lobe on her cranial ridge. These injuries are consistent with the damage of a domestic assault. Her partner nearly killed her.

CASSANDRA: You're—correct.

ALISON: You're surprised.

CASSANDRA: Yet not wowed. She remained unconscious though surgery relieved cranial pressure. And scored a twelve on the Glasgow. Tell me more.

ALISON: She underwent your procedure despite that worrisome score.

CASSANDRA: She wouldn't be my patient if she hadn't. Observations trump deductions, Dr. Montour.

ALISON: With respect, that was an observation. The scars on her cerebral cortex are unusually pronounced, injuries unique to your procedure. She required maximum stimulation to recover.

CASSANDRA: With respect, such detail isn't available at this resolution.

ALISON: There's visible discolouration near—

CASSANDRA: Perhaps your keen focus is best drawn to more important details.

CASSANDRA manipulates the scan in a huff.

7. Ne-haa-wa-pu-wuh [Danger]

The hospital music-therapy room: MEGAN *paces, psyching her-self up. She approaches the audience, as if they were her friend.*

MEGAN: Hey, newbie. I—I wished more people would've checked on me. But who could take—imagine, seeing me often. I—damn it. I'm talking like I'm in therapy.

Let's. Do. Coffee.

You've gotta deal with your shit.

Don't cry. We're buds. And I don't want to catch syphilis. Go fuck yourself.

She storms across the stage. Club lights animate the scene.

MUSIC: Fierce techno.

She dances. She looks suggestively over her shoulder, as if she's noticed someone cute. She winks.

Hello, Mr. Saturday.

8. Ma-ta neh-win-ki a ne-kis-kow [Never Meet Your Heroes]

Star Trek *lab: Click.* CASSANDRA *triggers a video, to continue her grilling of* ALISON.

PROJECTION (recording): A comatose MEGAN *lies prone, dressed in a hospital gown. An* EEG *skullcap connects her with a digital piano and a computer.*

The skullcap hums as CASSANDRA *plays Mozart's Piano Sonata No. 2 in* F *Major,* K. *280, Adagio.*

MEGAN sits up, dazed.

PROJECTION (brain scan): The picture-in-picture image ends. Only the brain is seen.

CASSANDRA: Early data suggested we'd repaired her injuries. She soon had episodes of severe anxiety. Despite our pleas, she returned home rather than remain an in-patient. Every psychosocial assessment suggested she wouldn't harm herself or others. She never missed an appointment but her sessions became impossible. Hence my request for your insights.

ALISON: The patterns in her brain suggest significant long-term emotional trauma. She had a brutal life, long before this injury. That history, along with the damage to her cognitive centres, make conventional talk therapy risky. It could trigger flashbacks, violence, suicidal ideation—

CASSANDRA: Don't admire the problem. I want the answer. In words she'll understand. She's not a neuroscientist.

ALISON: Her spirit's calling for relief. Yet her brain only understands torture. Whatever medicine she chooses, be it a ceremony or Western talk therapy, she juggles a knife.

If she catches the handle, whew. If she palms the blade, ouch. The key is to engage neural pathways she hasn't tapped into. Her traditional language, supplemented by expressive arts and targeted electrical stimulation will instigate—

CASSANDRA: No techno babble.

ALISON: Lenape and creative therapies will use wiring that won't upset her. As gentle electrical currents develop healthy brain patterns.

CASSANDRA: How surprising. Another variation of the treatment du jour.

ALISON: You must be sick of people cribbing your methods.

CASSANDRA: Explain your modifications, beyond the addition of language.

ALISON: *(makes a fist)* Your method: coma victim. You play music. Add electrical stimulation. Mega zap.

(slaps her fist) Bye bye coma.

CASSANDRA: I requested simplicity. Not comedy.

ALISON: I have a point.

(points at slapped spot) It's red. Your mega zaps leave scars. As terrifying as that sounds, a brain can work around them. You revive someone, have a few check-ins to make sure they're okay, they go home. Everyone's safe, if they only receive single treatments. My

patients are traumatized. I can't help them with a single procedure. If I used mega zaps each time, I'd kill them. I lowered the current—

CASSANDRA: To permit multiple sessions.

ALISON: But my mini zaps aren't strong enough to repair damage without additional sources of stimulation. I added Indigenous language, music, and visual art, to activate pleasure centres and vital cognitive regions. My patients developed healthy neural pathways.

CASSANDRA: No one's less Indigenous than me. I don't understand why you connected my methods to yours.

ALISON: Sometimes life hits us too hard, too fast, too often. Wham. Misery makes our brains function like they're damaged. We can't recover. Your work mends wounds that forget how to heal.

CASSANDRA: Key-hoo-le-nee-uppy-soo-way?

ALISON: I didn't catch that.

CASSANDRA: My patient demanded a helper who could answer her. If you can't, I'll find someone who will.

ALISON: She wondered if you speak Lenape. I think. Your pronunciation's off.

CASSANDRA: I assume you aren't mocking me.

ALISON: Pish. Te-he-ti. [I am. A bit.]

CASSANDRA: I'll need a translation.

ALISON: Whatever struggles she's had post-treatment, you saved her life.

CASSANDRA: Offering platitudes is the surest evidence a doctor has no idea how to treat her patient. "She'll make a full recovery" is the only acceptable sentiment here.

ALISON: She'll make a full recovery.

CASSANDRA: Perhaps not. Your panic attack made the rounds on social media. My patient won't be impressed.

ALISON: Trust isn't an option for a woman this traumatized. If she doesn't see that video, something else will happen. She'll threaten to sue. Call me dirty names. It's a test. She needs proof I'll support her at her worst. I will.

CASSANDRA: You fled a worthless conference. If you flee mid-treatment, she dies.

ALISON: Ma-ta neh-win-ki a ne-kis-kow. [Never meet your heroes.]

CASSANDRA: We've established I don't speak your language.

ALISON: My apologies. Sometimes Lenape helps me sort my thoughts. I meant to say I've attended ceremonies, therapy, workshops, yoga, talking circles—

CASSANDRA: Yet you're beyond agitated. Don't pretend otherwise. Such distress might confirm your instability.

ALISON: Or frustration. Colonization, suicide, violence, substance abuse. I'll never list all my community's scars. Our damage gets attention. Never our healing. I doubt non-Indigenous people read my work.

CASSANDRA: Dr. Alison Montour, International Journal of *Indigenous Health*, volume twenty, issue three. You tested 202 subjects.

186 of them recovered. A success rate rivaling my own. But none of your patients had trauma you deemed medically impossible.

ALISON: I'll adapt my methods.

CASSANDRA: You seem sure of that.

ALISON: Hope isn't hope if it's subtle.

CASSANDRA: Hope's only necessary when we fail.

9. Boom

A shitty bachelor pad: MEGAN *pats an empty bed with a come-hither glance.*

MUSIC: Sexy make-out tunes.

She draws her hand across her chest to invite her snag's touch. She notices the letter in her bra.

MEGAN: Never mind this thing. Tell me what turns you on.

SOUND: A punishing slap.

10. Ne-chee-puh-tay-na-muh-wuh [I Thought I Killed Him]

Star Trek *lab: CASSANDRA's grilling of ALISON continues. They lock eyes.*

ALISON: It seems anything I say will set off a bomb.

CASSANDRA: My patient will have you dance through a minefield. I'm simulating her pressure. I must be sure you won't break. Again.

ALISON: I've invited you for coffee, lunch, name it. If you'd accepted, you'd already know me. And my capabilities.

CASSANDRA: We had no reason to meet. Your work lacked merit. Until your most recent study.

ALISON: Kindness works as well as pressure.

CASSANDRA: Yet everyone isn't kind.

ALISON: You've made that clear. I'd be out the door but I've seen this scan. She needs help.

CASSANDRA: It remains my task to determine your capabilities. And I have another concern. Your critics deem you incapable of functioning in a scientific world or an Indigenous one. They're certain you've united the world views to hide your clinical deficiencies in both.

ALISON: Critics don't matter. My skills do.

CASSANDRA: I'm calling your bluff.

CASSANDRA powers up her digital piano for a simulation.

PROJECTION (mannequin wearing EEG headset): It lies prone like a coma patient.

Click. CASSANDRA activates the headset.

SOUND: It hums.

My team must practice. Sadly, few volunteers sign up for aggressive brain manipulation. This set up is the next best thing. We play; algorithms predict how a damaged brain will respond.

CASSANDRA hammers a sour note. All video goes dark. The hum stops.

If we err, a fail-safe device shuts everything down. A handy feature, until I must reboot.

CASSANDRA flips a switch on the EEG headset.

SOUND: The hum resumes.

An override switch shortens restart times. I've set the difficulty to maximum. I, and I alone, succeed at this level. But not often.

CASSANDRA hits a computer key.

PROJECTION (mock brain scan): Red and yellow.

ALISON plays Rachmaninoff's Piano Concerto No. 2 in C Minor.

CASSANDRA rolls her eyes like a teacher ready for a student to fail.

PROJECTION (brain scan): It becomes progressively red.

ALISON alters her tempo and frantically pokes the screen.

PROJECTION (brain scan): A brief flash of green.

SOUND: A beep.

CASSANDRA checks the readings, flummoxed.

There has to be an error.

ALISON checks the screen, also surprised.

ALISON: He's awake. Ne-chee-puh-tay-na-mu-wuh. [I thought I killed him.]

CASSANDRA: You know I didn't catch that.

ALISON: I'm glad he's well.

CASSANDRA: The computer told you to play "Piano Man." You changed the music. You should've failed.

ALISON: My sister Steph was an actress. She played Juliet, a year before she died. The balcony scene—she never felt so alive. The director scored her work with Rachmaninoff. It felt like better medicine than Billy Joel.

CASSANDRA: Some might question the risk of using intimate emotions while providing treatment.

ALISON: Back home, we speak from the heart. Or no one listens.

CASSANDRA: Where I'm from, actions matter.

ALISON: Like not panicking. While you beat me to a pulp.

Lights out, except a spotlight on CASSANDRA and ALISON.

CASSANDRA swears under her breath. She reluctantly offers an ID tag/fob.

ALISON snatches it with glee. She exits to celebrate. CASSANDRA faces an unseen BERNARD.

CASSANDRA: I'm aware of the incident at FredSpeaks. I hit her with everything. There's no one else.

PROJECTION (BERNARD's lips): He smirks.

END OF PROJECTION.

11. U-mu-shoosh-shum [My Wife]

Star Trek *lab: CASSANDRA's eyes droop as she reviews ALISON's treatment plan for MEGAN.*

AUDIO: Raucous classical music streams on her computer. It's stimulation to help her stay awake. The song becomes Mozart's Piano Sonata No. 2 in F Major, K. 280, Adagio.

CASSANDRA: Melanie's favourite.

Her eyes sag with such exhaustion her head follows. Her eyes snap open. They close again. Her head nods. She's asleep.

(hallucination; recorded) Yes, love, I should rest. I know I've already approved the care plan. I have to be sure Dr. Montour won't kill Megan.

I've run the data six times, if you must know. Sleep's optional until I've completed a seventh check. I'll join you when I can.

Yes, I wish you were alive.

She snaps awake. She sobs. Her tears continue, abating as the music takes her. The lights shift.

The space becomes a hotel lobby with a public piano. She plays it.

MELANIE swans in, a neuropsychologist, mid-thirties, who gets what she wants through any wealthy nerd means possible.

MELANIE: That's beautiful, Dr. Barry.

CASSANDRA: I'm Cassandra. Dr. Barry's my father. And my mother.

They're physicians. I am too, though they sneered while I pursued a doctorate in psychology after my residency.

MELANIE: It sounds like you've played your whole life.

CASSANDRA: My parents were aware of the correlation between studying music and high-grade point averages.

MELANIE: They were disappointed you studied psychology. Yet raised you based on psychological evidence.

CASSANDRA: Neuroscientific evidence. My annual presence here assures them I'm focused on hard facts, not touchy feely social science.

MELANIE: I hope you're enjoying the conference. Even if some delegates seem—touchy feely.

CASSANDRA: Neuroscientists are—competitive. I normally feel—out of place. I enjoy—how this feels.

MELANIE: The dinner's tonight. Please tell me you'll be there.

CASSANDRA: The banquet room lacks a piano.

MELANIE: Schmoozing should never come between a musician and her art.

CASSANDRA: I'm no artist. I—get flustered if I'm—fond of my company. Playing helps me—

MELANIE: Talk.

CASSANDRA: Not now. But generally.

MELANIE: Let me ask you something. I give terrible advice.

CASSANDRA: Me too.

MELANIE: Your doctorate's in psychology.

CASSANDRA: Neuropsychology. I'm a student of the brain. Not behaviour.

MELANIE: You have a musician's soul—don't deny it. You're the cuddly half of our dyad.

CASSANDRA: Something's troubling you.

MELANIE: I have a new friend. She's brilliant yet awkward. I think she's flirting. You know how it is. You must get hit on all the time.

CASSANDRA: Because women think, "She owns four cats and dresses like a mom. Swoon."

MELANIE: Maybe people hit on you and you don't even know it.

CASSANDRA: Uh huh.

MELANIE: Yep.

CASSANDRA: Dr. Laurier seems fond of you.

MELANIE: She doesn't play Mozart.

Lights shift, obscuring MELANIE.

CASSANDRA awakens. Her eyes lock on MEGAN's brain scan.

CASSANDRA: Someone needs me, love.

She kisses her fingers. She presses them to the piano, in MELANIE's absence.

12. Heh fuck face [Hello Fuck Face]

The shitty bachelor pad: MEGAN *glares at her attacker.*

SOUND: *Snoring.*

She grabs an empty beer bottle.

MEGAN: Bleed.

SOUND: MEGAN *shatters the bottle on her attacker's head.*

The lights crossfade, transporting her to the hospital music room. She dives across stage to her baseboard whisky, her entire body vibrating with distress. Gulp, gulp . . .

That was Saturday.

(gulp) This is therapy.

CASSANDRA: *(off stage)* The music room is on the right.

MEGAN *hears them, mid-sip. She stashes the bottle, a nanosecond before* CASSANDRA *enters with* ALISON. *Both are unaware of her distress.*

MEGAN: Hi, Cass-hole.

CASSANDRA: Please use my proper name.

MEGAN: Cassandra, Cass-hole. My injured brain's making connections. That's a good thing.

CASSANDRA: You needed something I didn't provide. Today's a step forward.

MEGAN: *(to ALISON)* You must be the miracle I've been waiting for. I'll call you Fuck Face. Ke-hu-loo-neh-soo-wa? [Do you speak Lenape?]

ALISON: Pish. [Yes.]

MEGAN: Ma-ta ell-ah-mal-sue-ha-leh-weh. [You can't be a real doctor.]

ALISON: Ne-tak-tahl. [I am.]

MEGAN: *(to CASSANDRA)* This doesn't erase your screw ups.

CASSANDRA: Every choice I've made is about your comfort. Including our change in venue. My office might feel cramped with three of us.

MEGAN: You wanted extra space, in case I got violent.

CASSANDRA: That sounded like a threat.

MEGAN: I won't get better in jail.

CASSANDRA: The less resentment you carry, the better you'll—

MEGAN: You woke me. Nothing you've done since has helped. You've failed in every friggin' way. Oh, shit.

CASSANDRA: Breathe, Megan.

MEGAN: You tried. You—it's not your fault I'm—me.

CASSANDRA: We'll help you.

MEGAN: Bite my ass. You can't even tell I'm fucking with you. This time, I have a witness. Piss off.

CASSANDRA bolts.

ALISON: Dr. Barry—

MEGAN: Screw her. I'm your patient.

MEGAN bolts.

ALISON: Megan—

13. Me-pow-huh [I Failed Her]

CASSANDRA's office: She white-knuckles MEGAN's file. She slams it on her desk.

MEGAN: *(recorded, distorted)* You failed in every friggin' way.

ALISON enters.

CASSANDRA refuses to look at her, hiding her shame.

CASSANDRA: I hope you settled her.

ALISON: I can't tell.

CASSANDRA: Close enough.

ALISON: You didn't deserve that send off.

CASSANDRA: Megan would disagree.

MELANIE: *(recorded, distorted)* That's beautiful, Dr. Barry.

SOUND: Tires screech.

14. Nah-kuh-loo-wuh [I Must Help People]

An ornate psychiatrist's office: CASSANDRA *bounces off the walls while sitting in place. Her foot taps. She shifts side to side. She locks eyes with the audience, as if they were her doctor. She tenses every muscle.*

CASSANDRA: A car wreck left my wife in a coma. Doctor after doctor failed her. They offered platitudes. "I understand your frustration, Dr. Barry." "Your wife's fighting, Dr. Barry." Melanie needed help. I read a news article, about a grandmother with a comatose granddaughter. The child's favourite song came on the radio. Gran climbed into bed and sang along, holding the young one. The child woke up. Encouraged, I put a keyboard by Melanie's bed. And played. She didn't recover. Music wasn't enough. Literature indicated that electrical stimulation showed promise. Her brain failed before I could target the current. I almost stopped my work. But I imagined someone else, hearing platitudes while the love of her life—

My procedure saves lives. One patient struggles. One. My work must continue. But the medical director's a monster. If word gets out I'm here, he'll call me a risk. "One error, Cassandra. That's all it takes." Caution remains my priority: if there's any hint my judgment's compromised, I'll—

15. Ma-ta lenape [No Lenape]

Star Trek *lab:* ***ALISON*** *radiates peace, her calm apparent as she organizes paints and brushes.*

MEGAN *explodes into the room, seized by a hulking rage.*

MEGAN: You're a fuck-faced panicking twat.

ALISON: You've googled me.

MEGAN: Cass-hole owes me a real doctor.

ALISON: E-kah-ski ah-len-eh-si wisk-tel-in-weh-si. [English feeds rage.]

Wham! ***MEGAN*** *kicks a chair.*

MEGAN: My foot thinks in English. Maybe you should call security.

ALISON: Ma-ta pe-shu-e-ka-ku-ne. [I won't.]

MEGAN: Speak English.

ALISON: Ka-toosh-kun Lenape ki-keh-wee-chuk. [You wanted to speak Lenape.]

MEGAN: I'm not wasting my language on you.

ALISON: Kuh-chi suk-we-leen-tuh-mu-hun. [You're worried I'll crack when you need me the most.]

MEGAN: I should've called you Einstein instead of Fuck Face.

(sneers at art supplies) I see you've been finger painting, like the other smart girls.

ALISON: Ke-noon-dee-hoom ke-nu-tu-neh-hue. Keh-tah-con ah-ween kaa-wee-hee-waw wee-knee-ska-pee-ek-wawa wok ke-shu-he-wow. [No medicine heals every wound. Music and visual art reach the brain where language can't.]

MEGAN: Hmm. Castle Dawn General Hospital. That's in Ontario. Save your hippie bullshit for British Columbia.

ALISON: Non nee-ew-tee-wah BC. [I've never been to BC.]

MEGAN: Speak English or I'm gone.

ALISON: You requested a Lenape helper so you could fire Cassandra. Knowing full well one might not exist. Maybe you wanted to give up. Maybe you needed care you weren't getting. Either way, I hope—

MEGAN: You're what happens when doctors get a tan and call themselves Indigenous. Go to hell, you colonized twat.

ALISON: Yep, I'm embarrassed.

MEGAN: I called you a twat. And you're joking it away.

ALISON: I thought you were being funny.

MEGAN: Everyone means it when they call you a twat.

ALISON: No wonder I live alone.

MEGAN: I'm not laughing, you piece of shit.

ALISON: Piece of shit. Ouch.

MEGAN: You're not injured. Don't swear.

ALISON: Some patients think a session feels more human if I curse.

MEGAN: Maybe you swear because you suck.

ALISON: Tell me how therapy should work.

MEGAN: "Tell me about the punch, Megan. Tell me why you drink. Tell me." You want my story, I get yours. Tell me why you fix people.

ALISON: Sessions are about you.

MEGAN charges for the door.

My parents left the rez for work.

MEGAN stops.

We spoke Lenape at home. Otherwise, Mom raised us like other kids. They played soccer, we played soccer. They studied piano, we—my sister and I hated lessons. We didn't see the Creator's plan, until Mom volunteered at a senior's home. She was proud of us. Recital proud. "Come hear my tiny monsters."

Forty people showed up. One was a stroke patient. Her face was paralyzed. We soon played "Let It Be." Mom teared up. She sang. Everyone sang—everyone. Even the stroke patient. It's no secret art heals us. But this was our art. We weren't stuck in piano lessons to fit in with white kids. We—made someone happy. I couldn't stop.

MEGAN: You didn't shake. If you'd told the truth you would've lost your mind. *(as terrified therapist)* "What if I'm sharing too much?"

MEGAN extends both middle fingers, bound for the exit.

ALISON: My sister's dead.

MEGAN stops.

My story was true. I just—held back. Therapy didn't reach Steph. Elders were kind. She kept struggling. She finally—she did everything. She suffered anyway. Now I help people who lose hope.

MEGAN: Here comes Fuck Face saying what I want to hear. You read my file. To study how to screw with me.

ALISON: I'll be fired if you leave. You'll have nothing left but Cassandra.

MEGAN: Bitch.

16. Ah-ta-moom-beel [The Car]

CASSANDRA's office: She roars at ALISON during a debrief.

CASSANDRA: You required blackmail to keep her there. Of course you need a better approach. And your choice has me gobsmacked. Talk therapy might harm her. Yet you're forgoing expressive arts to offer—

ALISON: I'm happy to brainstorm options.

CASSANDRA: Each idea will require thorough research to verify their utility. Megan doesn't have that time. Come prepared with multiple recommendations. Substantiate each with evidence. Or get out.

ALISON: Then I stand by my revised option. While expressive arts show more promise, I can't proceed without her consent. Preliminary data suggests she can tolerate talk therapy for a session or two, despite the risks. It'll give me time to build trust. Hearing Lenape will also be soothing. I'll reintroduce expressive arts—

CASSANDRA: She refused to speak Lenape.

ALISON: I'll try again. I'm sidestepping, not retreating.

PROJECTION (hallucination): An overturned car.

End of projection.

CASSANDRA: If something goes awry, it's your last session.

17. Kwe-kwun-dah-seek [A Pill]

Ornate psychiatrist's office: A jittery CASSANDRA *evades the gaze of her unseen helper.*

CASSANDRA: She would've had Mozart cranked. It drew horrified stares from teenagers. The window would've been down, to maximize the breeze on her head. She called herself a mad scientist. She loved looking the part when she reached the office, her hair wild. It made her colleagues laugh. I've had to brush it out of her face, numerous times, to avoid—

The drunk swerved, not Melanie. Yet here I am, wondering if her hair was in her eyes. Damning myself, because I wasn't there to move it. I—your tedious smirk has returned. Some high-powered insight has you ready to pounce. Spare me. I know what's happening.

Like you, I see patients confess sins that never happened. Because it's easier to face imaginary crimes than reality. I'm—evading the reason I'm here. I've—never had visual disturbances. Medication seems prudent.

18. New-wee-kox-kuh-wuh [My Sister]

ALISON's cheap, tiny loft: She jabs a keyboard with woodpecker-like speed and ferocity as she inputs final data.

Click. PROJECTION (brain scan): A red amygdala.

Click. PROJECTION (brain scan): A red hypothalamus.

She records her thoughts.

ALISON: *(into smartphone)* Cass-hole's—Dr. Barry's—refusal to collaborate has forced me towards a problematic option. Data suggests the use of Lenape, without additional stimulation from other sources, won't temper Megan's trauma response. Her notes indicate she's refused multiple referrals to ceremonial supports due to her religious upbringing. I don't want to risk alienating her by suggesting them again. Creative therapies remain a strong option for generating healthy pathways. Yet she'd rather play lacrosse in a hurricane than use expressive arts. Her demeanor resembles Steph's, before she—

PROJECTION (hallucination, river): A swift moving current, not yet at whitewater rapid pace.

ALISON draws a fearful—no, soothing breath. The river disappears. The sound of the water continues.

She jams her EEG headset over her skull and triggers a PROJECTION (video): A recorded ALISON comforts her onstage counterpart.

(in video) Every time you do the procedure, the river feels more like medicine.

On stage, ALISON *plays Rachmaninoff's Piano Concerto No. 2 in* C *Minor, 2nd Movement on the digital keyboard.*

(in video) Steph stood—

On stage, ALISON *freezes the video.*

Steph.

19. Beethoven

Star Trek lab: ALISON and MEGAN struggle through the session. MEGAN sits within arm's distance of the digital piano.

ALISON: I don't know how to say "drugs" in Lenape. If you had heart surgery without anesthetic, you'd die. But some therapists rip on with no thought of the pain you'll endure. Tell me what heals you, not what harms you.

MEGAN: You're giving me therapy. To help me recover from therapy.

ALISON: Chi-pa-taught-kway heh-mook-we. Neh-shisha keh-shi-teh-see. Ah-men-chi-ha ma-noon-keh-tun-hay. Sum-ton-he-yok. Ma-tah-con-chi-hell-ah. Ni hach new-wha-too ma-ta ki-ke-oh-kan. Kwi-cheh-mulch. [Helper after helper had my sister reliving her agony. By the end, nothing made her as suicidal as a session. Awful therapy took everything from her. It mustn't hurt you too.]

MEGAN: Beethoven.

ALISON: I don't follow.

MEGAN: Beethooooven heeelps me relaaax.

ALISON: Nah-you-wee-wah hee-lit nee-ska-pii. Kee-kaye-heh-weh— [We have a library. You can stream music—]

MEGAN spins to the piano. She nails the first notes of Moonlight Sonata.

MEGAN: *(as she shows off)* —I. Play. Piano. *(winces; flubs a note)* When my useless brain works.

20. Kweh-chee-wuh-lee-he-tool [Fix It]

CASSANDRA's office: She attempts another supervision session with an excited ALISON.

ALISON: I'd no idea she was trained.

CASSANDRA: Nor I. Not that her musicality had relevance while I treated her.

ALISON: I wasn't implying you missed something. This is my way in. I'll—

CASSANDRA: Your enthusiasm confuses me. She felt nauseous. She expressed frustration with her playing. Such irritation could deter her from your plan, not draw her to it.

ALISON: Few musicians have used a gaze interface. The novelty could sway her. Playing piano without striking a key will confuse her, create neural pathways. Positive images shown mid-procedure will ensure those pathways are healthy. Look.

Click. PROJECTION (brain scan): A green brain.

Bingo.

CASSANDRA: *(as she inputs data)* Injured brains hate novel stimuli. If hers responds with distress—

Click. PROJECTION (brain scan): A red brain.

ALISON: Could you suggest refinements to—

PROJECTION (brain scan): The car wreck appears on the image.

CASSANDRA: You missed a key variable. Do your job. Or I can't.

21. Mozart

MEGAN's living room: One dollar Mr. Noodles containers smother her space, except the area around an electronic keyboard.

She removes the letter from her bra. She reads it, a tear in her eye.

MEGAN: I miss you too, Trudy.

She stuffs it back in her bra.

She taps a key on a digital piano. Then another.

MUSIC (recorded, distorted): Mozart, Piano Sonata No. 2 in F Major, K. 280, Adagio.

A red wash covers the stage. She screams.

SOUND: An ambulance siren.

22. Ma-chee-yay [Grief]

Ornate psychiatrist's office: CASSANDRA *evades her helper's—no, she locks eyes. Her body tenses, ready for a fight.*

CASSANDRA: My treatment of Dr. Montour shouldn't concern me. Her incompetence might cost me everything. But my behaviour—I can't stop lashing out.

My frustrations are plain. Any failure with a patient becomes ammunition for Bernard to—

My funding's vulnerable. There are no other consequences, whatever therapeutic pish posh you're hinting at.

Enough. If I lose the clinic, I can't help anyone. And if I can't help anyone, there's nothing to hide my grief. That's what you want me to think.

Kiss my ass.

23. Ma-ta-ho-he-kway-soo-wuh [A Good-for-Nothing Woman]

MEGAN's room, psych ward: Her wrists are bandaged. Natural light makes her glorified cell feel like a glorified cell with natural light.

Thud. ALISON drops a file near MEGAN.

ALISON: Your notes.

MEGAN: Spoiler alert: I'm angry. Slutty. Useless.

ALISON: Went-ah-may-muh kah-ki-hen. [Nothing says you back down.]

MEGAN: Next time, give me a pep talk before I slit my wrists.

ALISON: Cassandra kee-coo lee-aw: "eh-en-tah-wee-sek keh-tah-lee-way-len-si kee-keh-oak-an." Pish. [Cassandra quoted you: "Scars mean less than healing." Agreed.]

MEGAN: Get out.

ALISON: Huh. My mind blanked on Lenape. My wiring gets mixed up when I'm stressed. I bet you understand. Sometimes your thoughts don't feel like your own. Sometimes you do things you'd never do. Then in the middle of that fog, the real you comes back, kweh-ti spung-weo-kun [for a second].

MEGAN charges, ready to fight. She freezes. She cries instead.

MEGAN: Zip. Left. Zip. Right. Boom, I was dying on the floor. Another

Indian who cut herself. I don't remember calling an ambulance. But I did it.

ALISON: I'm glad you're alive.

MEGAN: You said your mom whitened you up with piano. Promise me you weren't screwing with my head.

ALISON: I wasn't.

MEGAN: Those notes are right. I'm—useless. I spent a year in college, waitressing on the side. I was studying to help kids with messed up lives. I flunked. Ten years passed. No one asked if I'd give school another try. I'd hit my peak. One thing kept me from cutting myself: I taught piano, to welfare kids who couldn't afford lessons. To hell with that college. I was helping people.

I needed—to do something good. Uma put me in lessons, as a kid. She wanted me away from hand drums. The stuff God hated.

I loved Uma. She loved me. She didn't want me to hate myself. But playing shrivelled me. I became—someone else.

Teaching changed everything. You hear these stories, about brats hating lessons. Lots did. But some—they left, happy. Happy.

I can't teach. My head's too jumbled. Last night, I practiced to clear my head. I felt—fingers. They played a song. In my brain. Something's fucked. Something I can't fix.

(snatches the letter from her bra) This bullshit says I'm awesome. *(rips it)* I'm just a bitch who got punched.

ALISON reaches for the pieces.

Leave it.

ALISON: You keep it next to your heart.

MEGAN: Yeah, it's so important you never asked about it.

ALISON: Cassandra did. You got upset. Or so I read. I thought you'd bring it up, when you needed to.

MEGAN: Get away.

ALISON steps back.

I'm done spilling my guts. My story gets yours. That's how we work in Lenape country.

ALISON checks over her shoulder. No one's looking. She pulls up her sleeve revealing a vicious scar.

ALISON: Meh-keesh-hee-teh-hee. [I missed my sister too much.]

MEGAN: I should be talking to a ghost.

ALISON: Ah-peh-cheh-kooks-ki-heh-le ma-ta well-ah-si. [I refused to die knowing I could've lived.]

MEGAN: You made it. Tell me I will too.

ALISON: Ma-ta-pe-ta— [We're different—]

MEGAN: Different.

ALISON: Ne-shi-na-luk-wah. [I've hurt you.]

MEGAN: Speak English.

ALISON: We heal in different ways. That's all I meant.

MEGAN: You don't think I have a chance.

ALISON: Of course I do.

MEGAN: Then say it.

24. Noo-la-lus-ta-wee-wuh [I'll Listen]

CASSANDRA's office: Her seething contempt for ALISON erupts as screams and finger pointing.

CASSANDRA: Patients half as volatile as her destabilize when therapists reveal their own traumas.

ALISON: She opened up. That's more than anyone's managed.

CASSANDRA: She never hurt herself in my care.

ALISON: I've cleared every move with you. If you've had a better idea, I've never heard it.

CASSANDRA: My input's been ceaseless. None of which you've processed while you've read scans upside down.

ALISON: My inspiration thinks I'm a joke. You must've wondered why I've tolerated your contempt.

CASSANDRA: *(as ALISON)* "I can't leave someone in pain."

(as herself) I see through you. Without Megan, your work's damned to obscurity.

ALISON: I don't give a monkey's ass about awards. Or funding for my own *Star Trek* lab. Your care shaped her brain. My care has to gently build on yours. Or I'll kill her. Tell me every detail of your process. Find the error that left her a wreck. I can't fix your mess without you.

CASSANDRA: *(as she leaves)* Security will see you out.

ALISON: I'm not the one who should be dragged away. Your stagger gets worse daily. Your eyes are bloodshot, swollen. You look like you've been punched. And my god, I've never seen one staff member in your halls. They're hiding from the most confrontational soul cancer I've met. You've wondered if I could handle the pressure here. You're the last person I want firing electricity into comatose brains. It won't be long before administration agrees with me.

> *CASSANDRA slaps—no, she stops the blow, an inch from ALISON's cheek.*

I deserved that.

CASSANDRA: I restrained myself. It won't matter. The fact I wound up is all the ammunition you need.

ALISON: You never told me about your wife. Everyone knows she—and you turned that grief into a life-saving procedure. I've seen your worst. I should've remembered your best. I was an idiot to lash out.

We keep failing. It's killing me. I think it's killing you too. We can reach Megan if we stop fighting. There's more happening than what I know. Talk. I'll listen. Please believe me. I'll listen.

25. Wa-nah-kwa-tee-loon-dam [Grief]

Ornate psychiatrist's office: CASSANDRA *examines a potted plant, her visage available to her helper but not when tears are possible.*

CASSANDRA: Dr. Montour seemed—sincere. Her cautions were valid. I haven't slept well in days, weeks, I don't know. That's—no way to help.

Easing my burdens seemed the fastest way to pull myself together. I told the truth. And gave her approval to proceed as she must. But she didn't hear—

I can't shake a thought. Familiar music has better odds of success. I ask loved ones for suggestions. My patient arrived alone. I guessed. I thought of Mozart, Piano Sonata No. 2 in F Major. Melanie's favourite.

Let me finish.

If my playing was rueful, my patient could've sensed my mood.

I said let me finish.

Her distress might've triggered emotional centres responsible for traumatic grief. I could've overstimulated those areas. She might be in agony because I can't—

I'm not hiding behind my work. I'm confessing, damn you.

Melanie's head fit here. I massaged her scalp while she slept. I'd lean on the headboard, the perfect view of her face. I stroked her hair. She never woke. Yet I always made her smile. I'm still wired to reach for her. I can't let go of someone buried in my brain. I kissed her goodbye before the crash. I said I loved her. Yet we didn't make love. The delay might've saved her life.

I didn't request a ride, to steal more time with her. She would've changed her route. If she wasn't on that highway, she'd be alive. If the worst happened anyway, whatever I did, music could've woken her.

She didn't need a headset. All I had to do was play with more vigour.

Melanie got my best. It wasn't enough. My patient got my best. And my grief might've rebuilt her brain. Perhaps I haven't harmed her. Perhaps I'm looking for sins more forgivable than letting my wife—I don't know.

26. Pa-ta-ma-wee-wuh [Pray]

MEGAN's room, psych ward: she confronts an approaching ALISON with a sneer.

ALISON: Em-pow-loh. [I screwed up.]

MEGAN: Everything you touch turns to shit. Be specific.

ALISON: Uma ma-tah-ah-lah-si mem-hu-eh-soo. Uma nes-ko pem-uh-si. [Your Uma wasn't fond of our ways. I'm guessing she never learned Lenape.]

MEGAN: My cousin couldn't watch me shrivel. He taught me. When Uma wasn't home. And I still haven't heard how you pissed up.

ALISON: You listen to Lenape. But you rarely speak it. You were telling me something. My mistake was missing the hint. Keh-ta-len-eh-si ah-men-chi. Lu-nah-pay wu-sah-ken. Ni-ni-chi ay-li a-luh-nich-sia. Wok kesh-i-na-la Uma. [Our language is bitter medicine. It heals you. And it hurts you. Because speaking it to your grandma would've hurt her.]

MEGAN: I'll stab you if you tell me to hate her.

ALISON: Wul-hal-eg-lu-hay-na uhnk-oon-tay-wa-kuh. Wok wi-ta-ho-loa. Ah-pik-on went-ah-lean-heh-ka nut-ho-can. Tat-hen-too pah-tam-we-oak-ana nah-koo-tem. Ah-pi-kon wok puh-enema wok kul-he-haw-kwin. Weh-ka-ta-luck-weh pah-tam-weh-oak-an nah-kum-coon-on-ak, ent-hen wah-tah-ma. Weh-wee-new-wees. Wok ne-wee-kox-ke-wuh Uma. Neh-she-lin-tam. [She kept you from the old ways. But she loved you. Some kids played hand drums. You played a piano because she wanted it to bring you peace. However we make music, the Creator touches our hearts. I treated you like my patient. Not someone who's lost a gift. I'm sorry.]

MEGAN: Fix it.

27. Trudy

Star Trek *lab: ALISON adjusts the EEG headset worn by MEGAN.*

PROJECTION (MEGAN's brain scan): The readings blip.

An apparatus resembling a tablet rests on a music stand near MEGAN. A similar machine is placed near a piano.

MEGAN: You meant it. We're not drumming.

ALISON: Your prayer's different. Ma-ta-ke—

MEGAN: Use English. Lenape makes your hippie bullshit seem real.

ALISON plays Für Elise.

PROJECTION (brain scan): Green streaks MEGAN's brain.

ALISON: That's what Beethoven does to you. Painting and electrical stimulation will enhance the effect. Lock eyes on a note.

MEGAN: Cass-hole used a headset too. Look where it got me.

ALISON: This is different. I promise.

MEGAN looks, despite her irritated sigh. ALISON plays a C.

MEGAN: Piss off.

ALISON: The gizmo tracks eye movements. If you want a note loud, stare.

MEGAN glares.

ALISON plays a booming series of notes: A, F, and G.

If you want it quiet, glance.

MEGAN glances.

ALISON plays a soft B, D, and E.

MEGAN: *(as ALISON)* "Megan, the gizmo makes me a Jedi."

(as herself) Shove it up your ass. I cut myself playing music. Now you have me playing music. When I snap again, I'll press an inch deeper.

ALISON: Pah-tah-meh-weh-oak-ana me-keh-moh-se-wah-kan pah-tah-ma. [Prayers need faith.]

MEGAN: Friggin' Jedis.

ALISON: I'll monitor your readings. One hint of trouble, we'll stop.

Kesh-ah-tam, may puh-way-now ah-pik-we. Meh-pen-ah-si. Keh-weh-pen-ah-si— [Remember, if you want a note loud, stare. If you want it quiet, glance. Loud, stare. Quiet—]

MEGAN: I get it.

MEGAN stares.

ALISON plays "Twinkle, Twinkle, Little Star."

You guessed.

ALISON: Stump me.

The song morphs into Beethoven's Sonata No. 8 Op. 13, 2nd Movement.

PROJECTION (MEGAN's brain scan): Yellow streaked with green.

MEGAN: My head feels weird.

ALISON: If it's a headache, we should—

MEGAN: It doesn't hurt. It—tingles.

ALISON: Keh-tem-pem peh-wen-tow. We-che-mouw weh-la-mal-se-wa-kan. [Your brain's creating pathways. Pick up the brush.]

MEGAN: Screw your hippie shit.

ALISON: Nah-hu-mi. [Trust me.]

A hesitant MEGAN grips the stylus resembling a brush.

Lik-seh-men meh-wek-ah-nay. [Paint a dog.]

MEGAN: Like a kid.

ALISON: Na-hu-mi. [Trust me.]

MEGAN rolls her eyes but paints.

SPLIT SCREEN PROJECTION (scan/painting): The outline of a dog sketched by MEGAN's shaking hands appears stage right. The drawing crossfades with a five-year-old girl's self-portrait, walking a dog with MEGAN. A message is included: "Get well soon, Ms. Megan. I miss lessons. Love, Trudy." The brain scan burns red.

MEGAN: I wanted that letter in the friggin' garbage.

ALISON: Ah-pik-we mi-lan Uma. Woo-laa-pa-seh-kan: Trudy. [Piano was your grandma's gift. That gift brought your prayer: Trudy.]

MEGAN: Ma-nun-key-neh-kwe-hin. Ma-ta-ma-nu-kin-kwe-hin. [Everything comes out angry. Even if I'm not.]

SPLIT SCREEN PROJECTION (MEGAN's brain scan): It turns sixty percent green.

MEGAN hugs ALISON.

28. Teh-tuh-woo-nee-kees [The Police]

Hospital music-therapy room: MEGAN *checks for witnesses, ready to savour baseboard whisky.*

The piano catches her eye. She steps away from the bottle.

She plays a chord. She stops, awaiting panic. Still safe, she plays Beethoven's Sonata No. 8 Op. 13, 2nd Movement like a fifties rock song. Her blissful grin fills the room.

PROJECTION *(hallucination, river): Calm waters wind through a sunny forest. The ripple of the water blends with the music.*

She plays on.

Her music gets softer and softer. She closes her eyes, almost stopping as if hypnotized by the water.

The song becomes "Twinkle, Twinkle, Little Star." Twinkle, twinkle, little—she flubs the note.

MEGAN: It's okay to piss up the Mozart arrangements, kiddo. But you'd better nail your Beethoven.

PROJECTION *(hallucination, river): The water turns to rapids.* MEGAN *can't breathe. She pounds her chest, desperate for air.*

Projection ends.

SOUND: A mag lock opens. A police siren sounds. Police car cherry lights flash.

Help me.

29. Ee-hee-shaa-pa-muk [The Bottle]

Star Trek *lab: A beaming* ALISON *whistles as she inputs her electronic case notes. Her fingers dance.*

A somber CASSANDRA *enters.*

CASSANDRA: The police arrived with a warrant. They claimed Megan assaulted someone with a beer bottle.

ALISON: If they've locked her up, she'll—

CASSANDRA: She's already in a secure ward. They'll leave her be, until she's out of our care.

ALISON: I'll see her.

CASSANDRA: She's resting.

ALISON: Under sedation.

CASSANDRA: You can imagine her reaction.

ALISON: You should've talked her down.

CASSANDRA: She escalated quickly.

SOUND: Tires screech.

CASSANDRA goes silent, lest she reveal her distress.

ALISON: Unbelievable.

All lights blackout, save a spotlight on CASSANDRA.

MUSIC: *It continues, louder.*

SOUND: *Tires screech.*

CASSANDRA *can't breathe. She puts her head between her knees.*

SOUND: *Her cellphone rings.*

CASSANDRA: Call Dr. Whitmore.

Just do it.

PROJECTION *(on* CASSANDRA*): A car wreck.*

SOUND: *Tires screech.*

She screams.

30. Sii-poo-wah [The River]

Star Trek lab: *MEGAN undergoes treatment with ALISON's headset. She can't sit still.*

She stabs her paint brush into a canvas as ALISON plays Beethoven's Piano Sonata No. 30, Op. 109, 3rd Movement.

PROJECTION (MEGAN's brain scan): Occasional waves of yellow penetrate swaths of red.

MEGAN: Fucking cops.

ALISON: Your readings are wild. Maybe we should delay—

MEGAN: Nothing will fix me if I don't get this out.

ALISON: Pushing too hard might—

MEGAN: It's my friggin' session.

ALISON: Chit-ku-wi. K-si. [Be gentle with yourself. That's all I ask.]

MEGAN: Gentle won't fix me. You need to hear how I got hurt.

ALISON: Keh-tah-le-ni-he-si. [It's less upsetting to speak Lenape.]

MEGAN: I won't use it to talk about scum. You hear me—one word, I'm gone.

ALISON plays, one eye on MEGAN's concerning readings.

I've dated plenty of boozy assholes. That's who you meet, working in a bar. They stole from me. They banged my best friend. But they never hit me.

Tim washed my hair. When we went for walks, I'd find poems he'd hidden the night before, to tell me he loved me. But booze is funny. Drink too much, you're an idiot. Stop drinking, you're scary. He hadn't had a drop for a month, the night he—

I asked for him, when I woke up. I asked for him. The prick hit me so hard I didn't remember what happened for six months. Cass-hole helped me fill in the blanks. I didn't want her to. Tim, who washed my hair and wrote me poems—someone who loved me that much could hit me. I don't know where he is. He disappeared. I don't hate him. I don't love him. I want him to see what he's done. It's Wednesday. Trudy's class. We should be—

MEGAN gasps.

PROJECTION (hallucination, river): It rips across the stage, colliding with MEGAN's brain scan.

ALISON rushes to her.

It'll pass. Fix me.

ALISON: Nothing happens until I know why you can't breathe.

MEGAN: I see rapids. White water. It's already going away.

PROJECTION (hallucination, river): It roars across ALISON's face. Blink. It's gone. ALISON hides her panic.

ALISON: We—shouldn't continue.

MEGAN: Fix me.

ALISON: This side effect's—potentially treatable. But it's so rare, I might not understand it. I want you safe on the shore. Not in agony because I took a risk. We can try again. After I analyze—

MEGAN: You're shaking. There's something you're scared to tell me.

ALISON: I'm worried you'll storm out.

MEGAN: I'm still here. You're still shaking.

ALISON: Don't risk torture.

MEGAN: You said this was treatable.

ALISON: Potentially.

MEGAN: Potentially treatable. You wouldn't know that, if you haven't seen this before. You've fixed someone.

ALISON: One person. Without a brain injury. And she's still struggling.

MEGAN: But getting better.

ALISON: That could change.

MEGAN: You look good to me.

ALISON freezes.

(as herself) Your shakes gave you away. Cass-hole would have every kind of aneurysm if she knew you've screwed with your brain. You're scared I'll tell her your judgment's fucked, that I'm afraid you'll kill me. Don't deny it. Your lips aren't moving but your eyes keep talking.

(as panicked ALISON) "I use my gizmo to scan myself. Not for treatment."

(as herself) Huh. You've already changed your bullshit.

(as panicked ALISON) "I slashed my wrists. I needed special help. Therapists go to therapy. Doctors take pills when they're sick. The current's too gentle to warp my brain. I check myself, daily, to be sure. I'd never ask anyone to take medicine I wouldn't use myself."

(as herself) No one's gonna hear a word about this. If I lose you, I lose everything. Pain's made us sisters with the same story. You tried to fix yourself. And nothing helped. Except. Your. Friggin'. Gizmo. You need to worry about the other look in your eyes. Cass-hole had it too. Every time she knew she couldn't help me. You think I'm hopeless. So hopeless a machine that's fixed everyone it's touched—you included—won't work for me. You don't get to second-guess yourself. You don't get to leave me in pain. Your judgment isn't fucked. Your gizmo works. Use it.

ALISON: The gizmo works because I'm careful. Patience is medicine too.

MEGAN: I'll cut you.

ALISON: Please hear me out. When the river turned up, I panicked, for weeks. Water's a gift. Why was I seeing it as an attack? I couldn't find the answer in my data. I talked to an Elder.

MEGAN: Fix me or bleed.

ALISON: Her teaching frustrated me, like I'm frustrating you. But she was right. Every so often pain breaks us. We think we're useless, shattered. We miss the lessons in front of us. Here, right now, those rapids feel like danger. But if we heal, those same scary waters become a blessing. Once we're strong, and ready to help others, the river can rush us to anyone in need. Our neighbors, our brothers, our—sisters.

The silhouette appears. It reaches for ALISON *but it's trapped by the scrim.*

ALISON *chokes. Swift. Calming. Breath. Faster than a blink. The silhouette's gone.*

You mentioned Trudy. And you couldn't breathe. Sometimes our spirits reach out before we're ready. We end up terrified the best of us will drown. The key is to ease in, one step at a time. Not to throw ourselves into danger. Stay on the shore today. Admire the river. It'll take us to our loved ones, soon enough.

MEGAN: Every time we stop, the cops have proof I'm screwed beyond repair. And I rot, shaking in my room, waiting to explode. I didn't have your gizmo when I got drugged, restrained. I didn't have it when I slashed my wrists. I didn't have it when I tore someone's face off. Prayers need faith. I need faith that you give a shit. That you won't stop. No. Matter. What. Don't give up on me, like everyone else. I know the risks. It's my choice. Don't give up. It'll kill me.

A measured breath steadies ALISON. *She plays Beethoven's Piano Sonata No. 8, Op. 13, 2nd Movement with shaking—no, steady fingers as* MEGAN *paints.*

MEGAN *closes her eyes, easing into calm. She tries to speak. She can't. Note after note passes; she seems ready to cry.*

I wish I was Beethoven. When he was messed up, he wrote beautiful shit. I—don't do beautiful.

Last week, a prick ran away from a coffee date. Coffee. Something that stupid made me spiral. I ended up in a club, horny. I found a dude. Johnny? Dave? Mr. Saturday. I thought he'd be gone by Sunday. I didn't know I'd—the cops spent three hours grilling me about his scars. Three bloody hours. And a minute asking why I did it.

PROJECTION (stage right): MEGAN's scan turns deep red. She white-knuckles her brush.

ALISON: *(stops playing)* Megan—

MEGAN: Never. Stop. Fixing. Me.

ALISON plays on.

He wouldn't quit. I didn't know what he'd do if I fought. I let him finish. Afterwards, he passed out. This was my chance. I saw a bottle. I had to staple his face to my ass. He needed to kiss it daily.

He screamed. I smiled.

I smiled—because someone bled.

I'm buried. I can't be fixed if the best of me's smothered. Prison's a deeper grave. It doesn't heal.

SOUND: A buzzer.

PROJECTION (brain scan): A warning appears on the scan: "Safety levels exceeded."

ALISON: I have to stop.

MEGAN rips off her headset.

Projection of brain scans ends.

MEGAN: I should've known your gizmo's worth shit.

ALISON: Treatment takes time.

MEGAN: I'll have plenty of that in jail.

ALISON: You were assaulted. Anyone might lash out.

MEGAN: "Assaulted." Mr. Saturday'll say that too. "She assaulted me. With a weapon." What I did's different. Don't call it the same thing.

ALISON: He hurt you.

MEGAN: I can't prove it. He can show a judge the skin I cut off his face. I need proof I'm not dangerous. A brain scan, showing my head works. A report, saying I'm not violent. Your hippie bullshit doesn't have muscle. Cass-hole's gizmo, that's the ticket. It messed me up but she's a tool. If you're using it, blink, I'm normal. Erase my pain. Don't leave me a bomb.

ALISON: Treatment that strong can kill you.

MEGAN: I'm drowning, bitch.

PROJECTION (hallucination, river): Rapids smother them.

MEGAN exits, trapped in the current.

31. Neh-taa-wa-keen-ze-wuh [Read Carefully]

Star Trek *lab: Clack, clack, clack.* ALISON *inputs data, desperate, teary.*

SOUND: Squawk.

Damn it. She slams the desk.

ALISON: Ma-ta we-ke-me ne-kew-teh-lan. [She doesn't have time for me to get this right.]

CASSANDRA enters, holding a report.

ALISON uses every muscle to freeze in place, in lieu of throttling CASSANDRA.

I'm in no mood to argue.

CASSANDRA: I'm taking a leave.

Stunned. Silence.

ALISON: I don't know what to say.

CASSANDRA: *(hands report to ALISON)* You wanted a summary of my errors. My departure seemed easier if I wrote—my thoughts are likely malarkey. But I hope they help.

32. A-ween-dum [Pain]

Hospital music-therapy room: MEGAN *chugs her whisky. She hurls the empty off stage, every muscle still tensed by rage.*

CASSANDRA *passes by, upset.*

CASSANDRA: I didn't expect I'd see you. I'm tying up loose ends before I take time to—Dr. Montour can explain.

MUSIC (recorded): Mozart's Piano Sonata No. 2 in F *Major,* K. *280, Adagio.*

MEGAN *winces.*

I'll get a nurse.

MEGAN *hits* CASSANDRA *in the gut. She smashes* CASSANDRA*'s head off a table.*

CASSANDRA *goes limp.* MEGAN *steals her fob.*

33. Juliet

ALISON's cheap, tiny loft: She scrawls frantic notes on the report. Her eyes light up.

ALISON: Bless you, Cassandra.

She pounds data into her laptop.

SOUND: It squawks its immediate, negative response.

Smash! She slams the laptop on her desk. The computer dies, with an electronic static.

PROJECTION (hallucination, river): The rapids swell. Their audible roar is accompanied by the sound of panicked breath.

The silhouette appears on the balcony.

She grabs the EEG headset with jittery hands. She drops it.

SOUND: A distorted Rachmaninoff's Piano Concerto No. 2 in C Minor assails her.

She bawls, crippled by searing anxiety.

(recorded, distorted) Kweewihtoowen piiskeew nuskiinjuk,
Eel-nmaxkchaliingwehleewen
Eel-niakaanzhapptooneew wuulakwunuwii
Nawteepiilaweehkwusuwaw napsuweewaw: shukw
Nawulaaptoonaalaeew.
Kahwaaleewekw? Nweewiiheewekw kuwaw "piish,"
Waak nwulustaweewekw: shukw kpahtamaweewen,
Kmaxkalakayeew . . .

[Thou know'st the mask of night is on my face,
Else would a maiden blush bepaint my cheek
For that which thou hast heard me speak tonight
Fain would I dwell on form, fain, fain deny
What I have spoke: but farewell compliment.
Dost thou love me? I know thou wilt say "Ay,"
And I will take thy word: yet if thou swear'st,
Thou mayst prove false . . .]

She swallows a scream.

I won't quit.

She types hurriedly.

SOUND: An electronic crackle. Her computer malfunctions.

I didn't bust the simulator, you Best Buy piece of shit.

34. Nii-ska-pii [Death Music]

Star Trek *lab: MEGAN wears the EEG headset.*

She hits a chord on the digital piano: nothing happens.

MEGAN: C'mon.

SOUND: Beep.

Enter ALISON. Her jaw drops in horror.

(throws fob) Your boss sends her regards. Buzz security and I swallow my tongue.

ALISON: This isn't you.

MEGAN: If I die, I'm free. If I melt my brain, you'll rewire me. Either way, I'll stop hurting people.

ALISON: I can help you. Please believe me.

MEGAN: *(notices a switch)* —Oh. The safety.

SOUND: Her headset hums. ALISON pounces.

MEGAN hits a C chord. She collapses, near dead.

ALISON: No!

She slams a button on the wall.

EMERGENCY RESPONSE SYSTEM: *(recorded)* Code blue, Room 714.

35. Woo-la-pa-hee-see-kan [Good Medicine]

CASSANDRA's room, neurotrauma unit: the perfect place to recuperate. She soothes herself with music on her phone, gauze wrapped around her skull.

MUSIC: Mozart's Piano Sonata No. 2 in F Major, K. 280, Adagio.

CASSANDRA grips her head, dizzy.

ALISON enters, a huge file in hand.

ALISON: Melanie's favourite.

CASSANDRA: *(stops music)* You've read my report.

ALISON: You look ready to faint.

CASSANDRA: Thinking makes me nauseous.

ALISON: I'll go. I'd hoped you were in better shape.

CASSANDRA rips the document from ALISON's hands.

CASSANDRA: *(reads)* I was simply warning you to stand aside in case I vomit.

ALISON: Your headset will charge her auditory nerve, inferior colliculus, and auditory thalamus.

CASSANDRA: A song would pop in her head. Subconsciously.

ALISON: While the gaze interface shows her notes. When her pleasure centres react, I'll play. Her joy will intensify. Zap, she'll wake up.

CASSANDRA: Her tissue's too damaged.

ALISON: Her right frontal cortex, precuneus, left amygdala, and left insula weren't heavily stimulated. They may tolerate the procedure.

CASSANDRA: The answer was a blink away.

ALISON: I wouldn't have seen it without your report.

CASSANDRA: That report would've been needless, if her treatment didn't fail.

ALISON: I heard you didn't press charges.

CASSANDRA: My blunders mustn't harm Megan—again. You're grieving too. There's no margin of error. If there's any chance you'll hurt her—please keep her safe.

ALISON: Whatever our struggles, I never doubted you cared about her.

CASSANDRA: That sounded like a platitude.

ALISON: She'll make a full recovery.

CASSANDRA: If administration authorizes such risky treatment.

ALISON: If.

CASSANDRA: They'll approve.

ALISON: You seem certain.

CASSANDRA: Hope isn't hope if it's subtle, Dr. Montour—Alison.

36. Muh-lahn-dum [Vomit]

BERNARD's office: CASSANDRA wobbles. She glares into a PROJECTION (his eye): It narrows, as if focusing on the crosshairs of a rifle.

BERNARD: I hate reporting bad news while you're injured. Yet you insisted we talk. Your own words indicate that something as simple as your mood harmed a patient. The procedure's too dangerous to be performed in any capacity. Your clinic's operations will be suspended, pending a review.

CASSANDRA: I knew you'd bring out the noose. It's more troubling you're so predictable.

BERNARD: Your work means everything to you. Don't hide your woe behind snide remarks. Let it out, old friend.

CASSANDRA: I'll be fine. When Alison revives Megan.

BERNARD: Perhaps I wasn't clear. It's no secret you avoided Dr. Montour until every option was exhausted. Because you were aware of her floundering incompetence. If she proceeds, we'll smell Megan's brain fry from three blocks away.

CASSANDRA: You were breathing down my neck. I didn't give her a chance.

She wobbles.

BERNARD: You aren't well. Rest, old friend.

CASSANDRA: I'm not the problem you need to worry about, Bernard.

These are difficult times. Cuts galore. And multiple changes in leadership.

BERNARD: You're afraid I'm next. Because your injuries are connected to the malpositioned camera in the music room. The defect was never noted in monthly reports. The fool responsible will be terminated. More action will be taken, pending a thorough investigation. Fear not, my job's safe. I'll have a nurse assist you back to the ward.

She nearly doubles over, nauseous.

CASSANDRA: I look forward to learning more in court. You also didn't notice every page after the introduction was written in Lenape. Proof you're more concerned about shutting me down than reviewing a viable treatment option. Which includes mitigation strategies for the concerns you've identified. The proper report will be shared with our entire senior leadership. I'll attach a second analysis. Under your watch, 400 of 620 Indigenous patients were discharged with no treatment plans. Fifty of whom died homeless. Or you can endorse Dr. Montour's report to the medical advisory— Excuse me.

(vomits) What a mess, old friend.

37. Ma-ta-na-chi-moo-lee-wuw [Everything I Couldn't Tell You]

Darkness.

SOUND: CASSANDRA's version of the EEG headset hums in the dark. It vibrates the air.

Lights up.

Star Trek *lab: MEGAN lies prone. CASSANDRA's massive headset grips her skull. ALISON triggers the device from a laptop.*

PROJECTION (MEGAN's brain scan): It glows red. No change.

ALISON: C'mon.

She hits the key.

PROJECTION (MEGAN's brain scan): No change. ALISON blanches. She hammers the key.

PROJECTION (MEGAN's brain scan): No change.

Megan.

PROJECTION (MEGAN's brain scan): A brief flash of yellow.

Keh-pen-te. [You can hear me.]

PROJECTION (MEGAN's brain scan): No change.

PROJECTION (hallucination, river): It swirls around ALISON.

Kuh-chi un-kah-lu-hun, ma-ta sheh-shay-wa-nah-ku. Ma-ta as-hun-tays-heh-ha-tin. Kes-ki ta-li-cia. [This is the first time I'll speak to you, without a word of English. That's not miracle enough to get you on your feet. But it'll help you hear my heart.]

Ki-shell-ah-ma-lonk a-ta me-tea-ka-maw Lenape el ah-pik-we. Ne-shal-lam-we, na-hoo-ha-ni, we-chi-ah ne-chon-ne-stah-men. Ma. Keh-tah-con ah-ween kaa-wee-hee-waw wee-knee-ska-pee-ek-wa-wa wok ke-shu-he-wow. Wel-sit. Ki-che-mul, wok ke-ma-ni-tok-wah. Wok ma-ta-le-le-mi. [A whisper asked me to blend Lenape with Western art. I've spent years starving, ridiculed, wondering if I'd misheard. I didn't. Our language says you're beautiful. Their art reminds you some pain helps us heal. The Creator had me make medicine, just for you. But the hospital won't let me try again.]

Ma-ta-na-chi-moo-lee-wuw me-pe-kaa-ha-wuh. Ma-ta keh-neh-pwen tak-wun-da-may-wak. Ma-kii-she-eh-hay-een ne-tan-gee-loon-dom. Ka-ta wee-chuh-mul. Wok ma-ta keh—la-pi kne-wulch. Kwi-che-mul. Ka-ta-wi-chu-mul eel-we-cha-peek. Pah-tah-meh-weh-oak-ana me-keh-moh-se-wah-kan pah-tah-ma. [Everything I couldn't tell you is choking me. Sometimes the worst must happen. Our only relief is a hand to hold. I'll be here. Even if—I won't say goodbye. You're a fighter. You'll find whatever miracle you need. Prayers need faith.]

> *MUSIC (recorded): Rachmaninoff's Piano Concerto No. 2 in C Minor.*

(recorded, distorted) Kwee-wee-heh-too-wen peh-skew nusk-in-juk—[Thou know'st the mask of night is on my face—]

> *ALISON white-knuckles MEGAN's hand, choked by panic. She kisses MEGAN's hand. Her eyes close. She freezes, her lips still pressed against the hand.*

> *ALISON's entire body shakes in concentration.*

PROJECTION (animation): A cartoon ALISON kneels at riverside. White water rapids assail the shore. A tear falls from her cheek. It hits the rapids. The water calms.

Music ends. Animation ends.

Si-poo-wah ka-chi-pe-too-when wok ne-chi-tan-ee-si. Peh-meh-toon-ha-li. [Someday the river will carry you to shore. You're my sister now.]

MEGAN: *(recorded, distorted)* Ma-ta ke-nu-soo-me, wok Uma ton-kay-lan. [No one's cried for me since Uma died.]

ALISON grips the kill switch. She can't pull the trigger.

Ke-pen-tie. [You can't hear me.]

Ma-nun-key-neh-kwe-hin. Ma-ta ah-pik-we. Ke-tu-ke-nuke-weh. F and A flat, C, F— Ma-ta a-la! [Everything comes out angry. Even if I'm not. You're fixing me. F and A flat, C, F— Don't stop!]

A disconsolate ALISON pulls the—

PROJECTION (brain scan): MEGAN's auditory nerve, cochlear nucleus, and auditory thalamus turn green.

ALISON: *(rushes to piano)* Keh-mik-wi-ha. [Stump me.]

ALISON plays Beethoven's Sonata No. 8 Op. 13, 2nd Movement. One note, two notes, three notes—

Green illuminates the stage.

MEGAN bolts up.

Black.

Acknowledgements

These collaborators and loved ones offered personal or artistic support throughout the development of this work:

Brianne Tucker
Sarah Orenstein
Natasha Bean-Smith
Mac Hillier
Erin Brandenburg
Andy Moro
Jenny Young
Amanda Hyde
Kate Lewis
Deanna Choi
Michaela Washburn
Pip Bradford
Jiv Parasram
Pat D'Hondt
Jani Lauzon
Stephanie Belding
Cherish Violet Blood
Andrew Penner
Madison Walsh
Tara Everett
Rogue Benjamin
Elizabeth Morris
Gregory Oh
Meredith Henry
Carmelle Cachero
Lindsay Anne Black

The author wishes to particularly acknowledge Emma Mackenzie Hillier for her dramaturgical support. Anúshiik (thank you).

Jeff D'Hondt is a member of the Lenape nation at the Six Nations of the Grand River with additional Belgian Canadian ancestry. He has two decades of experience working in mental health and substance abuse treatment services, which he gained through positions in the correctional system, the Ontario Ministry of Health and Long-Term Care, within Indigenous communities, and at hospitals and homeless shelters. He graduated from the University of Toronto with an Honours Bachelor of Arts in History (with minors in Aboriginal Studies and the History of Science), from Toronto Metropolitan University with a Bachelor of Social Work (where he was also part of the contract teaching faculty), and from York University with a Masters of Social Work (where his research on using theatre to give voice to homeless Indigenous youth was awarded the Gerry Erickson Essay Prize for Best Practice Research Paper). He's also a K.M. Hunter Artist Award nominee who has written plays produced/workshopped in Toronto, Vancouver, and Los Angeles. He lives in Toronto.